Easy Answers
to Hard Questions

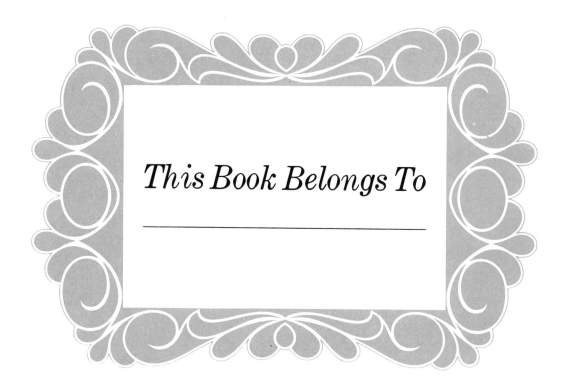

This Book Belongs To

_____

Easy Answers to Hard Questions

by SUSANNE KIRTLAND
Illustrated by SUSAN PERL

A Giniger Book
Published in association with
GROSSET & DUNLAP, INC.

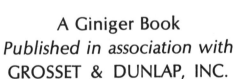

GROSSET & DUNLAP • Publishers • NEW YORK

INTRODUCTION

Parents, in their efforts to be parents and communicate with their children, need all the help they can get. This snappy, bright and factual book answers many (if not all) of the questions modern children ask, and will help to fill this need.

Too often when we are engrossed a child will demand an immediate answer to some "Why?" question. We often don't know what to say; we become angry and say, "Because." And some books to which we might refer tell more than the child wants to know.

This book is not meant to be a substitute for conversation, but should act as a catalyst to move parent and child forward in their daily relationship.

Who knows, a child might respect his parents more if he got these immediate, honest answers to his questions. Maybe parents ought to *memorize* these answers, and *really* impress their children!

Lendon H. Smith, M.D.
Member, American Academy of Pediatrics

1977 PRINTING
ISBN: 0-448-12409-2 (PAPERBACK EDITION)
ISBN: 0-448-03115-9 (LIBRARY EDITION)

Contents

What is the Earth Made Up Of?

The earth is a gigantic ball about 25,000 miles around. It has three main layers. The very center of the earth is called the core. It is made up of metals so very hot that some of the metal becomes liquid metal. The second layer takes up about 85% of the earth. It is made up of metals, too, but scientists don't know what kinds yet. The outside layer is the crust. About three-quarters of this layer is covered with water — oceans, rivers, lakes and seas. The other quarter of it is land where we live, and where grass and flowers and trees grow.

Why is the Sky Blue?

The sky looks blue because there is blue in sunlight. There are other colors in sunlight, too: red, orange, yellow, green and violet. But we only see these colors when raindrops separate sunlight and form a rainbow.

The earth's atmosphere separates the same way raindrops do. But the little pieces of dust and water vapor in the atmosphere reflect only blue, and not the other colors, and so the sky looks blue to us.

Why isn't the Moon Always Round?

It is always round. But the moon has no light of its own. The moon shines at night because it borrows light from the sun.

As the moon travels around the earth once a month, it seems to change shape, depending upon how much of the sunlit part is facing the earth.

You can watch the moon grow bigger and smaller. When the moon is new, you can only see a tiny sliver. When the moon is full, you see its whole round shining face.

Astronauts have made trips to the moon. Do you dream about going to the moon soon?

Where do Waves Come From?

Waves are mostly made by wind blowing on water. Wind separates the water into mountains and valleys. The mountains of water pour into the valleys to fill them up. This moving water pushes other water and makes it move, too.

That is how waves start. And the more the water travels, the bigger the waves grow. So ocean waves that travel thousands of miles are big and tall. And waves on ponds are very small.

What Makes the Wind Blow?

Wind is moving air. Air moves because of differences in temperature. Hot air is thin and light. Cold air is heavy. When cold air drops down, it pushes the hot air up, and a wind begins to blow. In March, strong winds blow umbrellas inside out and send kites sailing through the sky.

What Makes Thunder and Lightning?

Lightning is like a giant spark. It is caused by a kind of electricity in storm clouds. When storm clouds become full of this electricity, giant sparks flash out and leap from cloud to cloud.

When these sparks travel, they heat up the air around them. Air gets bigger as it gets hotter. As this hot air spreads out in the sky, it bumps into other air. This bump makes a big air wave that rolls around the sky. Then we hear the loud noise we call thunder.

What Makes it Rain?

Rain starts in a cloud, high up in the sky. Clouds are made of trillions and trillions of water droplets, tiny and light enough to float. When clouds get very cold, the water droplets freeze and get so heavy they can't float any more. Then they fall out of the cloud and melt on the way down to earth. That's what makes it rain.

When do We See a Rainbow?

We see a rainbow when there is rain and sunshine at the same time. Sunshine looks white or yellow, but it is really made up of six different colors.

When the rays of the sun pass through raindrops, the drops of water separate the light into all these colors. Then you can see a rainbow — bands of violet, blue, green, yellow, orange and red curving across the sky.

Where do Names Come From?

Thousands of years ago, when there weren't many people in the world, everybody just had a first name.

When the world became more crowded, many people had the same first name. It was confusing. So to tell all the different people with the same names apart, other words were added . . . and these words became last names or family names. Some last names told where people lived, what work they did, or who their father was. This happened in every country.

Do you know where your last name came from? And what it means?

Goldberg (German for Gold Mountain)

Cooper (English for a barrel-maker)

MacDonald (Scottish for son of Donald)

Palombo (Dove in Italian)

Where do Babies Come From?

Babies come from a special place inside their mothers. A baby begins as a small egg in its mother's body. This little egg starts to become a baby when it is joined by a tiny seed from the father. For nine months the baby continues to grow while it lives safely protected inside its mother. After nine months, a baby is still small — but big enough to live outside its mother. It is ready to be born. Most babies are born at hospitals. Some are boys and some are girls, but all babies are nice to welcome home as brothers and sisters.

Why are Some People Fat and Some People Skinny?

We get fat or skinny because of the different ways our bodies use the food we eat. Some children eat only a little and still get fat. Others can eat and eat and still be skinny. When we eat more food than we use in playing and growing, some of the food is stored in our bodies. This stored food is what fat is. Everybody has some fat. People who have only a little are skinny. And people who have much stored food are fat.

Why are People Different Colors?

Many scientists believe that when the world began, the color of people's skin was light or dark because of the amount of light rays they received from the sun. People who lived in cool cloudy places had lighter skin than people who lived in hot tropical climates.

Later, these people began to travel from climate to climate, so there are now people of all colors living in all parts of the world. They have inherited their skin color from their parents, just as you have. But no matter what color a person's skin is, everyone belongs to the same big family, the family of man.

What are People Made Of?

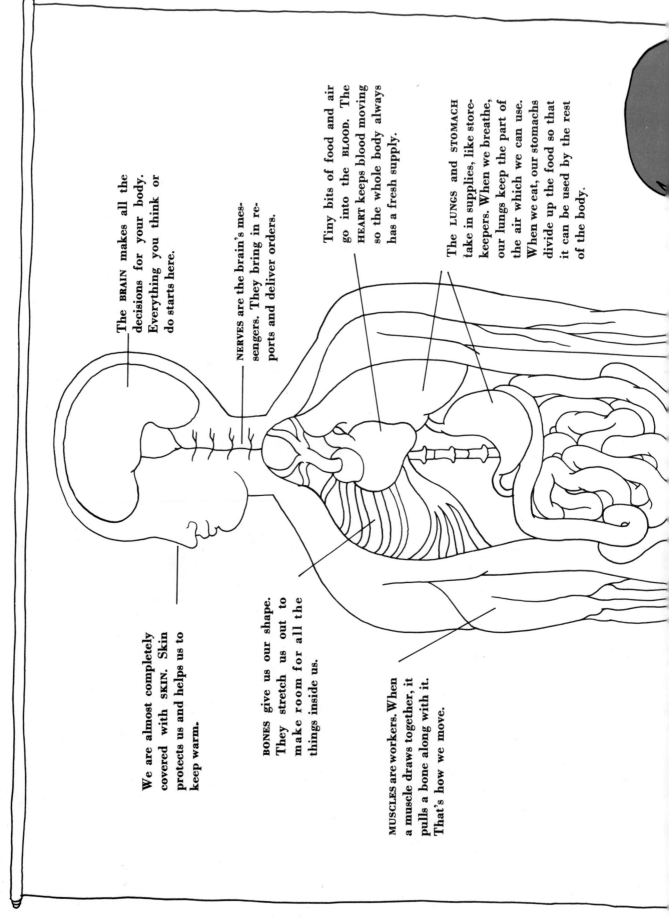

The BRAIN makes all the decisions for your body. Everything you think or do starts here.

NERVES are the brain's messengers. They bring in reports and deliver orders.

Tiny bits of food and air go into the BLOOD. The HEART keeps blood moving so the whole body always has a fresh supply.

The LUNGS and STOMACH take in supplies, like storekeepers. When we breathe, our lungs keep the part of the air which we can use. When we eat, our stomachs divide up the food so that it can be used by the rest of the body.

We are almost completely covered with SKIN. Skin protects us and helps us to keep warm.

BONES give us our shape. They stretch us out to make room for all the things inside us.

MUSCLES are workers. When a muscle draws together, it pulls a bone along with it. That's how we move.

The REPRODUCTIVE SYSTEM sends out chemicals that make boys become men and girls become women. As men and women, we use the reproductive system to make babies.

We're also made of things that nobody has ever seen: like PERSONALITIES and FEELINGS. These things are just as important as hearts and lungs and muscles.

Why do Teeth Ache?

As boys and girls grow up, their teeth grow, too. Sometimes this hurts a little. But when a tooth hurts very much, it means something is wrong. Teeth can get sick, just like any part of the body. Sometimes they grow too fast, or too slow. Sometimes they get pushed into the wrong place. And they can get germs, which make little cavities in teeth. When any of these things happen, you should go to a special tooth doctor called a dentist. He will make your teeth strong and healthy again.

Why do We Have Hair?

The very first people on earth did not wear clothes or live in houses, so hair originally gave men and women the same protection from heat and cold that it gives to animals. Today most people wear some kind of clothing and live in some kind of house. So, though hair still helps keep the heat of our bodies at an even temperature, most of us think of it just as decoration. That is why women like to put their hair up in rollers, and why men sometimes grow a beard or mustache.

Why do Some People Wear Glasses?

Your eyes are like little cameras. They take millions of pictures all day long. If some part of the eye doesn't work right, the pictures are fuzzy. Some people can't see faraway things, like street signs, clearly. Other people can't see small words in books. Different kinds of eyeglasses help all these people see things the way they should. And lots of people with good eyes wear sunglasses in the summer to protect their eyes from the bright light. Isn't it nice to know there are eyeglasses to help everybody see better?

Why do We Hiccup?

We hiccup usually because we eat too fast. Or laugh too hard. Then a muscle in our chests (called the diaphragm) starts to make quick jumpy movements. This causes the air we breathe in to go to the wrong place. Instead of flowing gently into our lungs, it strikes our closed voice box. And out comes that funny sound: HIC-CUP!

To help make those noisy hiccups go away, take a long drink of water. Or hold a deep breath. Or breathe into a paper bag.

Why do I Get Hungry?

Food makes your body grow and go. You feel hungry when your body needs food and your stomach is empty. Different kinds of food help your body in different ways. Some build strong bones, muscles and teeth. Some make your hair shiny and your nails healthy. Others are good for your eyesight. And some give you the energy to play all day. So, if you drink your milk and eat the meat, vegetables, eggs, cereal and fruit your mother gives you each day, you won't ever feel hungry — just healthy.

Why Must We Keep Clean?

Everybody's skin has millions of tiny holes in it, called pores. They are the exits for body oils and moisture. When we play and get dirty, the dirt gets mixed with body oil and perspiration — and fills up these pores. A bath with soap and water cleans pores out so these exits stay open to do their job.

Washing our hands before meals is important, too. All dirt has germs — and germs cause disease. If we eat with dirty hands, the germs can enter our bodies with the food. So everyone who wants to stay healthy, look pretty, and smell sweet must keep himself clean.

Why do I Have to Go to Bed?

You sleep to give your brain and muscles the rest they need so you can think and grow. Muscles take food from your blood and turn it into energy, so you can play all day. But your muscles get tired from playing. And your brain gets tired from thinking. A nap or a good night's sleep lets all these important parts of your body rest — so you have the energy to think and play again.

Why are Children Afraid of the Dark?

Sometimes children see scary things on television or hear a scary story before bedtime. These things aren't as frightening with the lights on and other people around. But when it's bedtime and we are alone in a dark room, our eyes cannot see as well. Toys and furniture become strange shapes in the dark. They can make spooky-looking shadows on the walls,

floor and ceiling. And our imagination makes us afraid of these different shapes and shadows. But when the lights are turned on again or morning comes, we see that what frightened us in the dark can't hurt us, because they are all things we know and love.

How do People Catch Cold?

We catch cold from someone else who already has a cold. When these people cough, sneeze, or just talk, they let tiny viruses (even smaller than germs) out into the air. If another person breathes these viruses, they can grow in his body. This causes the runny nose and aches and pains that we call a cold. When we do catch cold, we usually get over it in few days. And that's the best part: being well again, so we can go back to outside play.

How do Butterflies Fly?

Most butterflies fly with two sets of wings that shimmer in the sunlight like jewels. The wings swoop and loop in a figure-8 pattern, instead of just up and down. In America there are seven hundred different kinds of butterflies. Some fly high and straight, like tiger swallowtails. Others flutter. And skippers got their name because they fly in the same way children skip.

Why can't Animals Talk?

Animals can talk, but not the same way people do. Some animals talk by actions. When a bee wants to tell his family where to find food, he dances. Dogs use action and sounds to speak. They say hello by wagging their tails and barking.

Birds talk. When a robin sings, he's asking other robins to come visit. He chirps to warn of danger.

Whales, porpoises, and dolphins have their special underwater language — squeaks. Scientists have learned to understand these squeaks and speak them. Someday you may be able to talk things over with a whale, a bird, a bee, or a dog.

Where do Animals Go in the Winter?

In the winter, animals and birds have special ways of protecting themselves from hunger and cold.

Some animals, like woodchucks and certain bears, go into a deep, deep sleep called hibernation. They burrow into the ground, their heart rate and body temperature lower, and they live on fat stored in their bodies.

Many birds escape the cold by flying south. It is warmer there and easier to find food. Each fall they may fly thousands of miles to their winter home and then fly back again in spring.

Why do Leaves Change Color?

In the warm, sunny spring and summer months, leaves look green because there is a magical green coloring called chlorophyll in them. In the fall, cold weather and less sunlight make the chlorophyll disappear. Then we can see other colors that are in the leaves.

Beech leaves change from green to sunny yellow and orange.

Oak leaves turn milk-chocolate brown when the green disappears.

Maple trees have sugar in them. The cold autumn nights trap the sugar in the leaves and change them from green to beautiful purple and red.

Why do Flowers Smell?

Flowers smell pretty so bees and butter-flies will come and visit. Little capsules of perfume break open when a flower blooms. This sweet smell tells insects where the flower is. Insects get food from flowers. And flowers use insects to help make other flowers. So the per-fume helps them both. But some flowers don't have perfume. They attract in-sects just with their bright colors. And all flowers help make spring the sweet-est season of the year.

Jack-in-the-Pulpit has a sour smell that people don't like. But flies love it, and you can see them any hot afternoon buzzing happily around this flower.

The Morning Glory's sweet perfume fills the air on warm spring days. Lots of fluttery butterflies come to drink the sugary nectar.

Nectar is hidden far inside the Red Clover blossom. Its clean fresh scent attracts bumblebees, whose tongues are long enough to go deep into the flower and draw out food.

Why do People Work?

Most people work because working rewards them in some way. Usually, the reward is money, which helps us buy things: clothes, houses, food, vacations. But there are many other rewards people work for.

Some people work just for the good feeling they get by helping others.

School work is a form of work we do which helps us to improve ourselves.

Planting a garden is work, too. And the reward is seeing beautiful things around us.

What is Love?

When a friend asks you to give him another push on his kiddie-car, and it's the twenty-fifth push, but you do it anyway, that's love.

When your sister breaks your favorite toy and then wants some of your ice cream, and you give her three licks, that's love.

When you want to do something very much, and your mother and father have good reasons why you shouldn't, believe it or not, that's because they love you.

All human beings have certain very strong feelings called emotions. The nicest emotion people can feel is love. Love is the warm happy feeling we get when we like someone or something very very much. There are many different kinds of love and many different ways we show it.

When you feed and brush your dog, and make your cat purr, and give a squirrel nuts to store away for winter, that's love.

When you see wild flowers in a field, and don't pick them, but leave them there to grow and fill the world with beauty, that's love.

When you obey your country's laws and show respect for your country's flag so that you can be a better citizen, that's love.